Giggly-Wiggly, Snickety-Snick

written by ROBYN SUPRANER   pictures by STAN TUSAN

PARENTS' MAGAZINE PRESS / NEW YORK

Text copyright © 1978 by Robyn Supraner
Illustrations copyright © 1978 by Stan Tusan
All rights reserved. Printed in the United States of America
10 9 8 7 6 5 4 3 2 1
Library of Congress Cataloging in Publication Data

Supraner, Robyn.
   Giggly-wiggly, snickety-snick.
   SUMMARY: Introduces the concept of such descriptive
words as hard, soft, rough, smooth, and others.
   1. English language—Semantics—Juvenile literature.
[1. English language—Semantics] I. Tusan, Stan.
II. Title.
PE1585.S67   482'1   76-14406
ISBN 0-8193-0854-4   ISBN 0-8193-0855-2 lib. bdg.

*To Darren and Detrick Stewart
and the good times we had together*

*My special thanks to Henrietta Stewart
and to The Mother-Child Home Program of
the Verbal Interaction Project*

WHAT IS HARD?

The floor is hard. You can jump on it. You can stamp on it.
How HARD can you stamp?
A block is hard. It goes KLUNK!
That's hard. That's very hard.
A hammer is hard. It makes a hard noise.

BANG! BANG! BANG!

One thing about hard: YOU CAN'T SQUASH IT.

WHAT IS SOFT ?

A lamb is soft. Wooly soft.
A pillow is soft. Soft as a feather. Soft as sleep.
A kitten is soft. Furry soft. Purry soft.
Soft doesn't go KLUNK. Soft is like a whisper.
Tell me a secret. How soft is a whisper?
Oh, that's soft.

A soft word is *hush*.

WHAT iS BUMPY ?

Oatmeal cookies with raisins are bumpy. Lumpy bumpy.
Streets can be bumpy. Humpy bumpy.
A wagon on a bumpy street goes…
BUMPITY! BUMPITY! BUMP! BUMP! BUMP!
Baskets are bumpy. Bump up. Bump down.
Fists are bumpy.

MAKE A FIST. CAN YOU FEEL THE BUMPS?

What Is Smooth?

A baby is smooth. Soft and smooth. Nice baby.
When daddy shaves, his face is smooth. Nice daddy.
A sheet is smooth. Neat and smooth.
A bathtub is smooth. Slippery smooth.
Glidey. Slidey. Flippery smooth.
All over smooth.

S-M-O-O-O-O-O-O-O-O-O-O-O-T-H.

WHAT IS TICKLY?

Grass is tickly. It tickles your feet. It tickles your toes.
A feather is tickly. Tickly goes…
HA! HA! HA! STOP! YOU'RE TICKLING ME!
Mother's fingers are soft and tickly.
Giggly tickly. Wiggly tickly.
Tickly makes you laugh.

FIND A FEATHER AND TICKLE YOUR NOSE.

WHAT IS SHARP?

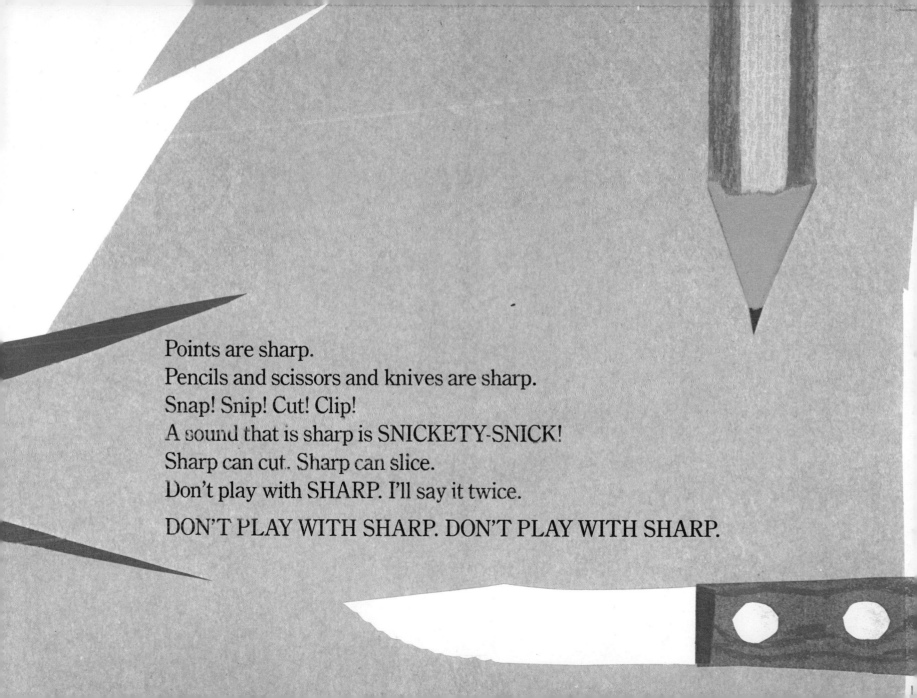

Points are sharp.
Pencils and scissors and knives are sharp.
Snap! Snip! Cut! Clip!
A sound that is sharp is SNICKETY-SNICK!
Sharp can cut. Sharp can slice.
Don't play with SHARP. I'll say it twice.

DON'T PLAY WITH SHARP. DON'T PLAY WITH SHARP.

WHAT IS STICKY ?

A bandage is sticky. Stick. Stuck. Sticky.
You stick to it. It sticks to you.
Jelly on your hands is sticky.
Lollipops are licky sticky.
Paste and glue are icky sticky. Ooey gluey.

STICK.   STUCK.   STICKY.

OOEY GLUEY

WHAT IS STRETCHY?

Sleepy arms are yawny stretchy.
Hands that reach for things are stretchy.
Tiptoe stretchy. Treetop stretchy.
Higher. Higher. Stretch and touch.
Rubberbands that p-u-l-l-l-l-l are stretchy.
Red and blue balloons are stretchy.
Blow one up and watch it grow. Big. Bigger. Biggest.

POP!

WHAT IS COLD ?

Ice is cold.

A snowman's face is nice and cold.

A glass of orange juice is cold.

An ice cube makes it twice as cold.

A cold word is BRRRRRRRRRRRRRR!

A cold thing to say is "I'M FREEZING!"

WINTER IS COLD. AND SO IS NO MITTENS.

WHAT IS HOT?

Fire is hot. The stove is hot.
Water in a pot is hot.
Boiling hot. Bubbling hot.
Don't touch HOT. It hurts a lot.
A hot word is OUCH!
The sun up in the sky is hot.
Sizzly. Frizzly. Sunburn hot.

A GOOD THING FOR A HOT DAY

IS LEMONADE.

WHAT IS CRUNCHY ?

Crackers are crunchy. Crisp and crunchy.
Celery is munchy crunchy.
Autumn leaves are crackle crunchy.
Crickle, crackle, day and night,
crunchies CRUNKLE when you bite.

BABIES CAN'T MAKE CRUNCHY SOUNDS

BECAUSE THEY DON'T HAVE TEETH.

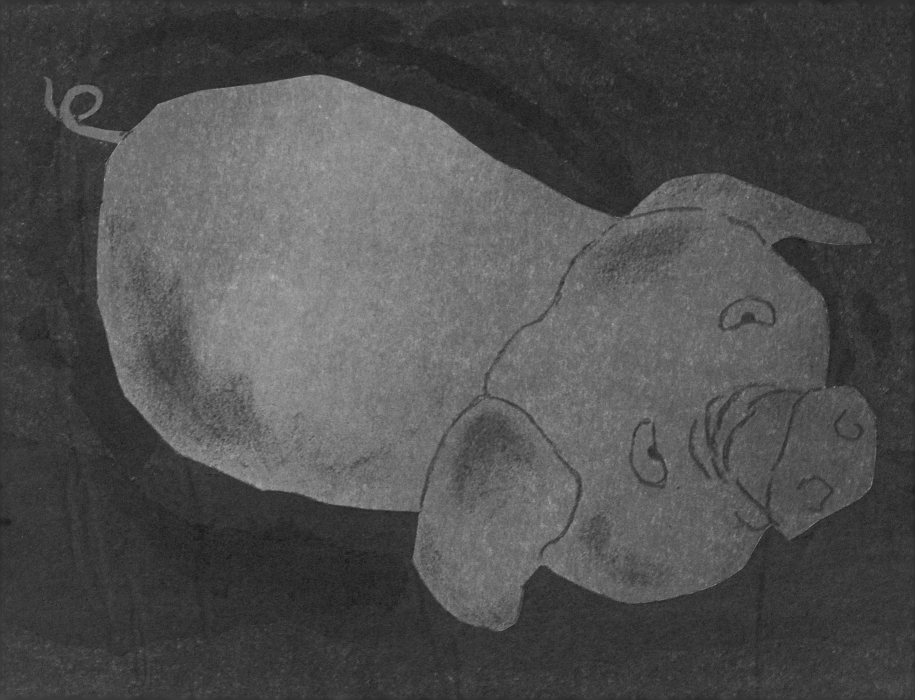

WHAT IS SQUISHY?

Mud is squishy. Mushy. Gushy.
Squish. Squash. Time to wash.
Fingerpaints are squiggle squishy.
Through your fingers. Through your toes.
Oozey. Goozey. Squishy goes SQUISH-SH-SH-sh -sh-sh-sh.
Squishy never goes CR-R-R-R-RUNCH!

A squishy thing to eat is chocolate pudding.
A squishy thing to take is a mud bath.
Oooooh. That's squishy.

WHAT IS FLUFFY?

A chick is fluffy. Feather fluffy.
Cotton candy on a stick is fluffy.
A baby duck is soft and fluffy.
Tickle fluffy. Powder puffy.

Clouds up in the sky are fluffy.
Wooly white and windblown fluffy.
A dandelion is huffy fluffy.

Huff. Puff. Dandelion fluff.

What Is Curly?

Curls are curly. Swirly curly.
Zingy. Springy. Curly as smoke.
A piglet's tail is twisty twirly.
Round as a ringlet. Pink and pearly.
Poodle pups and lambs are curly.

CURL! WHIRL! SWIRL! TWIRL!

Round in circles, little curl.

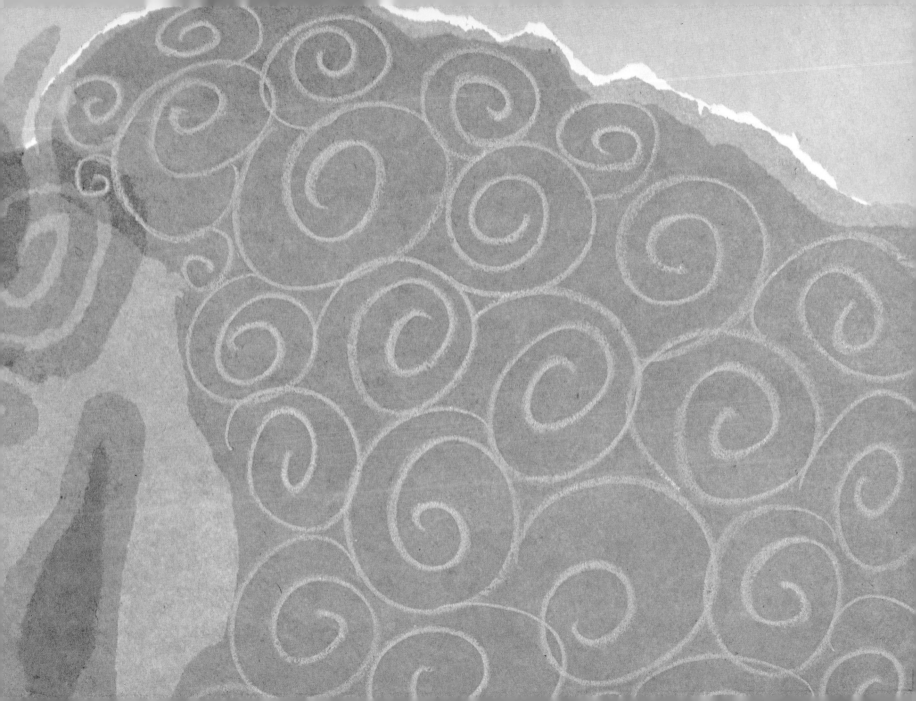

WHAT IS STRAIGHT ?

A ruler is straight. Straight up. Straight down.
Straight never bends or curls around.
Straight is strict.
Go STRAIGHT to bed! Come STRAIGHT inside! Look STRAIGHT ahead!
Straight stays on an even track.
It goes straight there and comes straight back.

Now, stand up straight. Very straight. Very, very straight.
Oh, that's good! COME STRAIGHT TO ME AND GET A KISS.